BEFORE VIOL

Joe Carrick-Varty is a British–Irish poet whose work has appeared in the *New Statesman*, *Granta* and *POETRY*. His debut book, *More Sky*, was named a Best Poetry Collection of the Year by *The Irish Times*, won an Eric Gregory Award from the Society of Authors, and was shortlisted for both the T.S. Eliot Prize and the Michael Murphy Memorial Prize. His second book, *Before Violence*, is a Poetry Book Society Recommendation.

Before Violence

Joe Carrick-Varty

CARCANET POETRY

First published in Great Britain in 2026 by
Carcanet
Main Library, The University of Manchester
Oxford Road, Manchester, M13 9PP
www.carcanet.co.uk

A CIP catalogue record for this book is available from the British Library.

ISBN 978 1 80017 542 6

Book design by Andrew Latimer, Carcanet
Typesetting by LiteBook Prepress Services
Printed in Great Britain by SRP Ltd, Exeter, Devon

MIX
Paper | Supporting responsible forestry
FSC® C014540
www.fsc.org

The publisher acknowledges financial assistance from Arts Council England.

Supported using public funding by
ARTS COUNCIL ENGLAND

CONTENTS

IN THE LATE FOREVERS

Drive This Tired 13
Snow 14
90s, Baby 15
Will This Train Take Us Home? 16
Legend Has it 17
Factual Pain Music Viewed from the Round Window of a Submarine 18
But Ryan Gosling Will Die One Day and the Trees Are More than Certain 19
What Does a Month of Sundays Mean? 20
Almost Back Where We Left Now 21
After Years I Start Dreaming 22
Old Poem 23
I Pick Myself Up with My Precious, Blood-Stained Objects 24
By which the Sea Means 25
The Mockingbird Fires 26
Beautiful People Sleeping Soundly Empty Mansions 33
You Will Have Your Body Soon 34
Only the Air Knew What We Had Done 35
A Future is a Collection of Bodies 36
Would it Not be My Prerogative to Bury Him Here? 38
Good News 39
And Then the Sky Pulls Up in a Silver VW Polo 42
In From the 90s His Body is Trudging 44
For Those Waiting and for Us Who Waited 45
People Die When You're Not Looking 46
In Memory of My People 48
Trees 49

Nothing and Nowhere is Only Itself 50
Home Alone Trying Not to Eat 51
A Brief Final Outing 52
Sibling Dream 53
My Father Follows the Years Down to the Lake 54
There We Go 55

BEFORE VIOLENCE 57

LATE FROM THE WATER 115

Acknowledgements 168

for us

IN THE LATE FOREVERS

DRIVE THIS TIRED

and when   the person
we were trying   to love
carried their   body
past all the   violent
picnics   of our lives
and when   from the
trees we   heard from
somewhere   deep inside
the bastard   hymn
of that slip   knot dream
the future   it knew
we were   suckers
brushing   crumbs from
a chequered   blanket
applying sun-   screen
to the   nth degree
our parents   they
teach us   how to die

SNOW

as if in the past it's about to snow
when snow doesn't exist imagine being
the night who first watched snow
or the lake who first believed it was
the night's doing there would be
history here rolling over in its sleep
imagine being the wind in that snowless
dream or the trees gathered like bodies
at the edge of the water i won't ask
what any of this means the snow
falls first through the sky into a dream
of history will you hear me this time
when i call your name through the snow
before it makes a white roof of the world

90S, BABY

for Caitlin

before violence   we were tiny
in the afternoon   of our longing
our parents kissing   near a fruit machine
we slept through Sun-   days on pub sofas giant
as the fields above cliffs   sister tell me
how old is the oldest child   in your body
how young is the last star   of its sleep
we were once so small   we fitted in the palm
of a sofa our father   was gentle
when he lifted our bodies   into the future

WILL THIS TRAIN TAKE US HOME?

parent kills themselves   during awful picnic
after long series of cumulatively   awful picnics
would not   be a bad way of describing
the yellow summer of my childhood   ask me
later and i'll give you a straight   answer
it's just   the tea is getting cold and there's
weather in my hands   weather in my face
such a pity there's weather at all   for a
second i'd like you   to imagine a weather-
less evening no history   attached to the
patio no future   fizzing in the apple blossom
when the nice therapist   from across
the Zoom call defines my   family
in such terms it's the word   exactly
which scares me   tell me what more
could your family have   done
what else did your family know   exactly

LEGEND HAS IT

shortly after i was born   my father
took me to visit   his father's grave
he carried my body   to the top of a hill
where his father   was buried
this story has become   a family legend
there was a time before   violence existed
in my family   this was not necessarily
during that time   at the top of the hill i cried
depending on who you ask   i was asleep
at the top of the hill   it was a Tuesday
or it was a Wednesday   my father was
between jobs   he wore a red puffer jacket
i slept for the duration   of the train journey
i cried   for much of the morning
my father held me high above   his father's grave
no witness   to corroborate events
i cried only when   my father held me
when he   put me in the sky

FACTUAL PAIN MUSIC VIEWED FROM THE ROUND WINDOW OF A SUBMARINE

there is no limit   to the amount of time
you can wait   for someone to die
but when they do die   just know
it will be your waiting   that killed them
believe it or not   there is a room
in your body   for every person you've known
and when a person dies   their room opens
and when their room opens   it tastes acutely
like   being fourteen and wanting
what you can't have   when my dad
turned sixty i took him   to the cinema
and between sips   of cider he'd smuggled in
he told me how   he never expected to live
this long   and then we just watched the film
and that statement got   real comfy
like the time   we got drunk together
after school and he told me how   last summer
he'd taken a shotgun   to a field and spent
a weekend deciding   whether or not he
wanted to be   alive on earth anymore
and the following morning   i was just
a kid hungover in assembly   sometimes
my dad looks like   a kid and sometimes
my dad looks like an old man   drinking
super-strength cider alone in his   flat on a
Tuesday it's true   sometimes i want to die
before violence   we were children

BUT RYAN GOSLING WILL DIE ONE DAY AND THE TREES ARE MORE THAN CERTAIN

after Sasha Debevec-Mckenney

he will die driving covered in   tattoos
and his body and the   corrugated wind
last summer   Ryan and i played a game
with the trees   we decided
they were well aware   of our bullshit
the fact we shouldn't   have been driving
Ryan changing gear and the   click click grrrrr
as the engine   held its breath
which Ryan   would come to tell me
was merely the sound of matter   changing place
like when a blue whale   yawns
and the lights go out in a   school hall
or like the time   i got a salary job
and my dad called me   middle class
and i believed   nothing would change

WHAT DOES A MONTH OF SUNDAYS MEAN?

i have a very small lake would you like
to help me move it from one end
of the garden to the other honestly
don't worry about the fish their sleep
is guilty and entirely its own problem
oh and the blue whales we get a few
of them pass through i'll take you down
tomorrow night do you ever worry
about shame blue whales are naked
even when they sleep i tend to just
walk around a lot did you know blue
whales sleep upside down like sky-
scrapers sunk hospitals tipped over
honestly most of the time i just want
to imagine the word Sunday picture it
in the water or failing the word
the smell of rain on Sun- day the hills
purpling above the garden all of this
more or less relaxed and OK and yes

ALMOST BACK WHERE WE LEFT NOW

knowing there will   be weather
and to be gormless   in its coming
it's summer and every-   one's upset
our friend running around   outside
of his body   isn't that what
we meant when we used   to say
happiness or experience   leaving
your person for a   brief moment
leaving even your head   your part-
icular interior landscape   replaced
by a tense in which   the future
so much further beneath   the surface
breathes like the promise   of the body
of a blue whale in a   David Atten-
borough documentary   when its cheek
grazes air   this television
is many times smaller   than the
whale's body beaming   light

AFTER YEARS I START DREAMING

it's always snow-   ing in my dreams
it was summer   when my father did his
awful thing   which doesn't make sense
because it never snows   in summer
when it snows at night   it's as if the world
is wearing earmuffs   was a statement
my father never said   every quiet roof
every hedge   sometimes it snows
inside my body   i am so stupid
winter   every year
surprises me   with cold

OLD POEM

in one of those poems   i wrote
in my early twenties   my father
would be arriving soon   over the back wall
as a bear or a bird   or a man older
than he ever grew to be   or perhaps
he'd arrive daily   only every day
he'd be younger until   our ages touched
until he was a kid   in my arms until
out of nowhere   the urge to hit him
would arrive   right here in this
rented kitchen   and perhaps
in the park later   i would hit him
the way he often   hit me in public
with the flat   of his hand on my nose
while a family of perfect   strangers
watched in silence   from a punt

I PICK MYSELF UP WITH MY PRECIOUS, BLOOD-STAINED OBJECTS

all year   i visited a dream
the dream   couldn't speak
the dream didn't know   its own name
or even that   it was a dream
i was a child   i had swallowed something
terribly important   like my father
or a piece of him   we were on holiday
on a beach in Lyme Regis   and the roof
of the holiday   was falling in
the sky   above my father's head
ripping in two   uncle T ruffling my hair
telling me   everything will be fine
but the dream   was not always like that
uncle T older   and more violent
his Spanish wife   leaving him
i loved the way   she said the word chocolate
dreams are like buses   was a thing
uncle T would say   before his face
fell off   and everyone stopped talking
i had not dreamt   in many years
i didn't believe   i was dreaming
on account   of the iceberg
we bumped into   on the steps
outside the   Southbank Centre
my Spanish auntie   managed a thing
my mother could not   she got away

BY WHICH THE SEA MEANS

is it bad   that all my poems begin
with the letter i   the sea doesn't
notice anyone   not even itself
when i first   became interested
in my family hist-   ory i asked
the sea for a map   away from
this beach   the radioactive picnics
had become   altogether too much
too many versions   of my family
steeped in   the afternoon with
no witness other than   the great
dumb sea   who had considered
my drowning   long before my
hereditary   what hope of a family
children of   my own running
around on sand   i would
rub sunscreen   on little backs
with the very   best intentions
look at my children   snorkelling
outside   of their lives

on the way back from the cinema   my dad asks
if we can stop at Tesco   and i don't ask what he needs
this late on a Sunday night   on social media
people i barely know   are winning prizes
and i'm hearting each post   as my dad shuffles across
the car park with eight cans of super-strength cider   hey
i wish i could make you better   i think with a squeeze
of his knee as the car sinks an inch or two   under his weight
i wish i could say   i am waiting for you to die
so i can kill myself   so would you hurry up already
all this dying   with nothing to show for it
back at his flat   the space between the sink and the oven
is filled with bags of empties   and like any good son
i take them down   to the big green bin

as i close the lid of the bin   i see Amash
watching through a crack   in the curtain
and i nod and he waves   and right then i decide
to do the least damage possible   for the rest of the week
which will probably look   something like
meditation and green tea   and cocoa butter on my shins
and saving for a flat   i'll likely die before owning outright
last year   when my dad got drunk and fell asleep
with a chip pain on   it was Amash who raced upstairs
with a bucket of water   before the windows exploded
and half the street lined up   on front porches
Amash kicked the door down   to find
my dad   standing in the kitchen in his dressing gown
a cabinet   melting off the wall

and we all know the rule   about chip pans
and buckets of water   just like we all know the rule
about love and knowing where to look   so when i pull
onto the street   i don't look up at the window
where i know my dad   will be leaning and waving
the same window that exploded   onto the street
a few weeks after the fire   when my dad
was out of hospital   we went for a pub lunch
and he said how lonely he was   and i said how precious
he was   cycling home i realised how little
i knew about him   how many questions
i still hadn't asked   how when i closed my eyes
and tried to picture him   he was always dead
in an armchair   with his mouth open
like he was trying   to catch rain

after the fire   the council re-housed my dad
in the ground floor   of a tower block
in the east of the city   the windows
were barred and painted shut   and the previous tenant's
ashtray was still on the table   when my sister
arrived with her friend   who helped move
everything that wasn't burnt   or black with smoke
i remember spending a Saturday   trying
to get internet installed in the flat   my dad
sipping cider the whole time   that evening
i asked for the address   of the Northside tenement his dad
was born in   i wanted to be certain
in the shower i opened a scab   at the top of my thigh
and watched certainty   go from red to pink to clear

my heart in the morning   is an intrusive thought
i've been having lately   it's one of the reasons
i can't do cocaine anymore   nights after a bender
when i become entirely aware   of my organs
i can literally   taste my heartbeat
the doors of muscle   opening and closing
last week i got a tattoo   of a blue whale on my arm
because blue whales   are conscious breathers
and when i was a kid   i'd lie awake for hours
breathing for myself   caught between
wanting to sleep   and not wanting
to forget to breath   which is what it feels like
when i'm sitting on the sofa   in my dad's flat
and the sofa creaks   and he's up for another can

growing up   my best friend’s dad was an alcoholic
as kids   we didn’t know he was an alcoholic
we just knew   he wore trackies and a rucksack
and when he took us fishing   he sipped
from a flask and smoked   and threw handfuls
of sweetcorn   into the water as my friend
picked at the grass and shrugged   this was before
my dad’s drinking got out of hand   or before
i understood   what his drinking would mean for us all
my friend was nine   when his dad died
alone in his flat   the neighbours complained
about a smell through the wall   just now my friend
calls from Thailand   he asks after my dad
tells me to sit with him   just sit with him he says

getting drunk at 11am   on a Tuesday is a way
of being certain   because if it's 11am and my dad's
got money   he'll be waiting outside the pub
with a guy called P   who every day without fail
arrives and leaves   on a mobility scooter with a bag
of special brew   swinging from the handlebar
but if it's 11am and he's skint   my dad will be sitting
at his foldout table   in his dressing gown
and it'll be raining   but he'll have the blinds shut
with the radio on   and the church bells will ring
eleven times   and like clockwork he'll crack a can
and he won't leave the flat   till his benefit
comes through   and here i am several cities away
i crack a can just to sit with him   to be alone together

BEAUTIFUL PEOPLE SLEEPING SOUNDLY EMPTY MANSIONS

you wake at 3am acutely aware   you have
swallowed something   important
or are in the process   of swallowing
in fact   you wake the very second before
the important thing finishes   its teetering
then vanishes   forever and it's like
one of those   bird's eye view shots
of a waterfall in a movie   a small boat
your important thing   the way
in this moment you begin   to dissociate
from your own body   gagging this slow
zooming out slow   panning away
and heck you think   this feels pretty good
and heck this emptying   this peace
of mind   and while sure there's a
part of you that's aware   that remembers
last night all the nights before   the tiles
cold   on your knees the tap running
your partner asleep   in the adjacent room
it's nice   to pretend it's nice to feign
newness to pray here   how weightless
a promise sliding back into bed   i'm sorry
you whisper   patting your belly running
a finger along a rib   now let me sleep
please i have paid my fare   O body
my important thing   i have offered

YOU WILL HAVE YOUR BODY SOON

all year   i visited a storm
the storm was ancient   the storm
like every storm   before it
was an iteration   of the first storm
it had rolled on   with its gusts
through many   violent afternoons
much clattering   in the trees
i was swimming   across a lake
my father a dot   on the shoreline
and the storm   was watching
or the storm was   inside my body
it's hard to say   we had come
to the lake as a treat   to make up
for an act of violence   and at some point
in all the excitement   i had swum too far
or i had swum   exactly far enough
my body   a pocket of weather
pushing out   across time
my body   high up somewhere
wanting the limit   of itself
O body   the things i will do
to make you   my own again
let's meet   in the middle
between violence   and the next
bout of   genuine happiness

ONLY THE AIR KNEW WHAT WE HAD DONE

when no one's looking i ask horses
at the edge of town to describe
in great detail what happened
to my family the grass replies
and every time only
the air thinks to listen

A FUTURE IS A COLLECTION OF BODIES

i sat at a window overlooking
a courtyard leading to a high wall
beyond which clouds and sky
i believed for this time that i was
on the ground that over the wall
was a city a Sunday market maybe
a street with families and a school
all the world's happening taking place
occasionally a bird would land
on the wall always the same robin
who watched me for a while
before disappearing occasionally
it rained and the window steamed up
with my breath sometimes the sky
felt close the clouds massive
and heavy like a person impossible
to love once during a storm
a blue plastic bag floated over the wall
landing in a puddle where it stayed for days
filled in the crevices with rainwater
that wouldn't evaporate i remembered
then a blue plastic bag swinging
from the handlebar of some long-
ago bike empty cans of super-strength
cider piled in a kitchenette it's not
that i knew who i was or where
my history was coming from
it's not that summer lifted
one day and all the violence arrived
all the dead ducks washing up
on the shore i climbed here

vents blowing steam   pipes sheer
and exposed   to die far away from
the people i loved   my life and my body
decidedly un-   horizoning those thin
years i survived   the green middle
of my twenties   to wake again
surprised   at the top of the sky
blinking the light   of this window
its courtyard and wall   and little robin

WOULD IT NOT BE MY PREROGATIVE TO BURY HIM HERE?

him being   the one
who put me   in nappies
put hands   on my mother
hands on himself   eventually
here being   the clearing
i arrive in   one morning
to begin this   slow act of
finishing the job   he started

GOOD NEWS

Dulwich Picture Gallery, 9 November 2022

1. A ROAD NEAR A POOL

the scene suicide creates   is entirely fictional
and carefully constructed   to lead our eye
around the room   the sloping
mountains unfold to   the pointing girl
who draws us to   the edge of a wide
pool where the person   naked
and shivering   kneels to drink
sometime soon   you will smell morning
and a parent will arrive   with clean clothes
in a duffle bag   yes there will be sky
but no sign of rain   the land will crack
but not here not now   stand with me
and look at your life   watch it appear
entirely accidental   the yellow pigment
which once   made the leaves green
disappeared   over time

2. VASE WITH FLOWERS

this bouquet could never have existed
suicide worked on the arrangement
over many months painting each flower
when it was in bloom you'll recall
the story about your nana floating
in her bathwater one Christmas
your dad the child lifting her body
your dad the child swallowing the end
of a shotgun all the times you've stood
high above a motorway wet railings
under your trainers the white rose
in the centre blossoms in the middle
of summer when the blue tulip above it
would have long withered

3. IN THE LATE FOREVERS

suicide takes us back in time   where
pyramids and peaks   are topped by suns
delicately supported bridges   connect rooms
contributing to the sense   of double horizons
where clouds or lightning   are not
where they should be   do you see
your body   curled in the corner
of the room   desert licking at the door
your sister   climbing back inside
your mum   whose broken nose
has bloomed   a butterfly
bruise behind   her sunglasses
your dad   as you always picture him
dead in an armchair   mouth open
like he's trying   to catch rain

AND THEN THE SKY PULLS UP IN A SILVER VW POLO

the sky announces   it has written a lecture
on domestic violence   no one starts a family
with the intention   of becoming
the violent dictator   of that family
we get inside the car   between drags
on a Silk Cut   the sky takes the register
we head deeper and deeper   into the desert
which i understand   isn't really a desert
but more   an immersive representation
of history   occasionally the sky stops
to collect a different   member of my family
i love how the sky   takes care
to lower   the accessible ramp
i want to reach around   the sky's
broad shoulders   i want to ask the sky
all my favourite questions   soon enough
the car is uncomfortably full   my nana
squeezes in next to me   she looks young
and sunburnt   and 100% not dead by suicide
she checks the buckle   on my booster seat
when our shoulders   smoosh together
i get a tingly feeling   because this
is the first time   that our skin has touched
i begin to worry   i won't have anything
interesting to say   about the sky's lecture
my nana tells me   to stop being silly
after some time we arrive   at a garden
giant eucalyptus trees   for miles
my nana leads me   by hand
to her favourite tree   remember she says
to find your tree   it's very important

i know without asking   that my nana
had to die   to find her tree
she loves the sound   of the wind
through its branches   i make a pact
with my future   i squeeze my nana's hand
but she's gone   just the wind prehistoric
and the sky   calling me back to the car

IN FROM THE 90S HIS BODY IS TRUDGING

on his back he carries   an invisible clock tower
in his hands he holds   the fourth summer
of my life i know   exactly what happens next
which is to say   i was old enough
to count the first time   i saw a ghost
my mother once des-   cribed the difference
between being dead   and alive

FOR THOSE WAITING AND FOR US WHO WAITED

for Caitlin

for the longest time we believed   our dad
would die   any second which of course meant
he never died   which of course meant we
killed him   over and over rehearsed his
dying   believed it had happened so many
afternoons cycled home   in a panic to hear him
snoring through the   letter box his death
our ritual in past tense   a childhood spent
waiting by a specific   pond the perfect
circle of which   my sister in jelly sandals
me shinpads up to the   nines tell us
do we look   happy waiting for our dad
to die   waiting as long as it takes
for his animal   to arrive
so that we might   one day
be children   again

PEOPLE DIE WHEN YOU'RE NOT LOOKING

all year i visited the ocean   we talked
about seasons   and about the moon
and the colour of rain   the ocean liked
to use itself as a metaphor   i was in a predicament
for a long time   i had been waiting
for someone to die   we talked about waiting
the ocean and i   waiting and dying
during one conversation   there was a cliff face
the ocean was time   there was damage
and a narrative arc   my father's dying had begun
as a secret   it was a private dying which meant
he carried it inside him   for many years
they say you're born   with your dying
folded inside your father's   breast pocket
or folded under your pillow   i can't remember
every hurt has its specific   number of wing beats
the ocean would drop fantastic   one liners
the problem is we were a family   there came a time
when my father   decided to have kids
when i was born   my father's dying went to seed
we were made complicit   first my mother and me
then some years later   my sister
there comes a time   the ocean would say
when a person's dying   takes on a life of its own
and it did   we were on holiday in Tenerife
we couldn't breathe   the ocean had convinced me
to try role play   a shark was floating by
my father was injured or angry   i couldn't tell
i lied to the shark   i smiled with all my milk teeth
until the shark wasn't interested   until it scarpered

a school fete radioactive   bunting in the
distance   soon we were outside
of our lives   we watched a cave being born
we watched him die   again and again
our house an aquarium   one bright afternoon
when i found him   chocolate biscuits
and medication   in his belly

so i'm at this party   and it's not just any party
it's a spider party   which is to say
everyone here is a spider   and not just that
i'm at a party with every spider   i ever swallowed
in my sleep   and we're all standing around
sharing anecdotes   until it's not a party at all
but a flat viewing and i'm   stepping into a room
someone died in   which must be such a normal
thing to do   to die in a room to die between
walls except i don't know this yet   i'll probably
never know   the estate agent describing the windows
the quality of light   at a certain time of day
and somewhere   a forest floor is becoming
very damp and somewhere   the shock
of a frozen lake and what if i told you a   secret
what if now feels   like the time to share
we're at a party after all   a spider party
and the vibe is actually decent   and yeah
maybe i'm drunk and brave   but look
a spider   is pouring Jameson and look
there's even a   beanbag and what if tonight
friends   my beautiful dead friends
we are alive   together again

TREES

if trees are the eyes   dead friends
see through   where is the mouth
to walk in a forest   is to grieve
within kissing reach   of a body
is to slip beneath   the green
middle distance   of grief i swear
i hadn't noticed   the trees before
you died   while i wasn't looking

NOTHING AND NOWHERE IS ONLY ITSELF

i looked down at a city   a bird landed
on the roof   of a tall building
i thought   how high this must be for the bird
on account   of the bird's body
being many times   smaller than my own
i was doing   that thing again
making the world   all about me
and yet the bird   was unperturbed
it was winter   in the world
so my staying power   glistened
from the surface   of the frozen river
which carved its vein   through the city
and yet the bird   ruffled its feathers
hopped on one leg   don't fall tiny bird
sadness is relative   you have no idea
how you'll feel   in a year
of course the bird   was just a bird
which meant   it didn't hear
my secrets   swimming around below
i stepped closer   to the edge of the sky
some gravel dislodged   every now and then
a secret would   rear its head
i would be drunk   and the giant shoulder
of one of my secrets   would graze the surface
much apologising   via text would follow
my friends would   look at me differently
some would slowly   back out
of the room   of my life
i asked the bird   to remember
a time   before violence
i don't know   just tell me anything

HOME ALONE TRYING NOT TO EAT

in order to make my problems   small
i take the chocolate brownie   to the middle
of a field in the middle   of the night
in the middle   of the hottest summer
in the UK on record   where the grass
tells me it has in fact   never been counted
where the sky tells me it has   in fact
never been to Tenerife   that's a different
sky altogether over there   and i feel
completely in control   of my life
for half an hour   swallowing tiny bites
of brownie in the middle   of a field
the uncountable grass   beneath
the immovable   sky

A BRIEF FINAL OUTING

all year   i visited a forest
the forest was angry   the forest
had been born   with an acute
awareness of   other people's pain
it would go   like this
a person would   slip inside
the forest's   green understanding
this was obviously   very difficult
the forest   was struggling
by the light   of a small fire
i listened   to the forest's heart
the wind moaned   through its blood
like the sound   of a distant train
on earth   it had been January
for a long time   in the world
of the forest's brain   we bonded
the forest and i   we watched a landslide
we watched   a family slip sideways
into the sea   behind our sunglasses
we nodded   this was our doing
by the light   of a fireworks display
the forest   turned to me
a bird melt-   ing in the corner
of its expression   we survived

SIBLING DREAM

for Caitlin

i feel a picnic lift   from its field
ripped like a scab   from the summer
of my body   i would describe the dream
i would describe   the events
in great detail   they say those who go mad
go mad   in the afternoon
in truth   nothing changed
we walked through   yellow light
to a picnic   we walked through
thick time   towards a group of families
under the sky   we played along
we took part   in the middle-
class activities   of the local area
nothing new   was discovered
no jacket mis-   taken for a tent
in the far-off wood   no dadless hour
stretched over the trees   when i wake
from the dream   i am relieved
i want to believe   it is true
that he succeeded   this time
that summer lowered   his body gently
and like that   he found peace

MY FATHER FOLLOWS THE YEARS DOWN TO THE LAKE

where he curls up   beside his dying
slurs his words   for one final voicemail
in the background   i hear wind
and the blue swoop   of a heron's wings
and the sky covering its eyes   like a son
high above my father's   naked body
with the island   of his face in my hands
i wish him   a swift drowning

THERE WE GO

when it happens   like nothing
romantic   when it's summer
and every   surface brims
with that late   forevers light
there is no   poetic aspect
no hill to crest   beyond which
my puppy fat   his suicide note
on the back   of a betting slip
look at us   carrying the meat
we are a coll-   ection of bodies
on its way   to a picnic
we are slathered   in sunscreen
and bucket hats   smiling
for the camera   like a family

BEFORE VIOLENCE

When I arrive at my death, I am either too tired or too sad to finish the job. I walk through every room, turning on all the lights. I find the Wi-Fi. My groceries are delivered by a man called George. We unpack the groceries slowly in the kitchen, George telling me how lucky I am, how he's the only member of his delivery team who knows how to find this remote cottage. I eat two ready meals and a Magnum and scroll social media for an hour.

I wake up with the idea for a poem on the tip of my tongue. It's the first idea, the first organic poem-making thought I've had in a year, and I panic, my brain full of static, and the idea disappears as quickly as it arrived. I feel the idea forgetting itself, breaking apart inside me. I open the curtains to a purple valley, a slate-grey lake, my first time seeing the landscape in daylight. My phone has run out of battery overnight so I've no idea what the time is. I get back into bed. I feel the mattress beneath me. I look at the ancient wardrobe, too big to fit through the door. I feel my body inside my life, inside the room, like a round window in a ship in a bottle.

I never know what to do with happiness. As a kid with a volatile, alcoholic father, much of my childhood was spent waiting for everything to go wrong. In this sense, you never quite relax. You live between moments of violence and love, your experience pooling in the dips of adrenaline between explosions. And this is how memory shapes itself: at an early age my memory moved from my mind into my body, and took route there. The lake of the mind and the lake of the body. One slowly giving, the other taking away.

When violence happens, it's often summer. There's a red taxi outside with the meter running and you can't find your tennis racket. You're panicking, digging through junk in the cupboard under the stairs, your father shouting from his bedroom. At first you don't register the punch, don't believe it, as it lands on your neck. Then another one lands on the back of your head, a cleaner connection this time, and you slam face-first into coats. Soon you will sit in a taxi as a city swims by. You will attend tennis practice. Kids will be acting like kids, running around on a court in bright sunlight. You will keep quiet, hit a few good balls. Your neck will stiffen. Life will happen to your body the way it always does: under the sky with nothing to say.

In the dream my sister is walking up a mountain. She's dressed for the beach, rocking jelly sandals and an Ireland bucket hat as she weaves her way through heather and sheep shit. It's one of those dreams where everything feels wrong, and it's one of those mountains that never ends. Each time she thinks she's reached the top, it's just another plateau and the next climb begins. Soon she's high enough to see into the next valley. A lake glistens. My sister sees other kids dressed for the beach climbing other mountains. It would be convenient to write something beautiful now. Like: isn't this how sadness must be traversed? In jelly sandals and a bucket hat. In a world where mountains are fathers slipped down from the pubs, their sleep a distant lake, medicated and rich.

Let's talk about secrets. What happens when you tell a secret? What happens to the secret? And what happens to the air in the room? Let's say the secret concerns a particular pattern of thought. Well, what happens to that thought when the secret is told? Does it unmoor? Lift in the silt? Sometimes I like to imagine my secrets as inanimate objects floating in outer space. Objects like, say, a kettle, or a tractor, or a house filled with a family. I spent my twenties writing poems about my secrets. Eventually I published a book of these poems. I held a launch party and invited friends and became invested in the idea of the book's success. I never intended for any of this to happen.

In the film *Honey Boy*, the protagonist, Otis, is in rehab for alcoholism and PTSD. Otis' father, a single, alcoholic parent, was violently abusive towards Otis throughout his childhood. There's a scene in the film, a flashback, when Otis' father begins to tell his son where he came from. The gist is that Otis comes from a long line of alcoholics, good people who suffered and used drink to hide their pain. My father told me something similar once. We were getting drunk together after school in a pub called The Crown. Near the end of the film, Otis asks his therapist: The only thing of value my father gave me was pain, and you want to take that away?

A year after I watch *Honey Boy*, I open social media to see a thumbnail for an interview with FKA Twigs. The post, captioned Singer-Songwriter FKA Twigs Alleges Abuse by Shia LaBeouf in First TV Interview Since Filing Lawsuit, has thousands of likes. I tap through to the article, scroll down to the video interview. FKA Twigs met LaBeouf on the set of *Honey Boy*. The film, written by LaBeouf, is a biopic of his childhood. LaBeouf plays his abusive father while FKA Twigs plays a neighbour in the trailer park. During the interview, FKA Twigs talks about the gradual nature of violence and abuse within a domestic context. How an abuser will, over time, subtly push boundaries until their partner loses any sense of themselves within the wider scope of the relationship. She also talks about love-bombing, how an abuser will predicate violence with love, threading genuine moments of happiness and relief, and how, as a victim in the throes of abuse, you live for this love before violence.

A few years after my dad moved out for good his drinking buddy M passed away. In the weeks leading up to M's death I sat with my dad in the pub, M a few tables away. It happens this way sometimes. Heavy drinkers, when they're near the end, will publicly give up. Their private chaos turning outwards: a skin of tiny, horrifying violences. When M shuffled back and forth from the bar I heard the rustle of the colostomy bag under his untucked shirt. He'd long stopped shaving. Stopped washing. I watched M take a long pull on his pint, and as he closed his mouth a strip of golden beer slipped out, landing with a splash on the table. Walking by the lake the day after M died my dad told me how, when his family had been taken away from him, M had been there as a friend. And it burned to hear my dad still thought of us in those terms, as things that were rightfully his. Our bodies belonged to the family. And the family belonged to him.

Writing that leans too heavily on autobiography. Writing that is revelatory in nature. Writing for the sake of revealing something hitherto unknown. Where the act of revealing takes precedence over the necessity of the work. How might this relate to shame? I am 29 and my body isn't mine. As a skinny undergrad, I walked out of the lecture hall thinking: I will kill myself before the age of 30. Is this such a strange thing to think? Strange to then text a friend? To eat crisps together on a bench outside the library?

During the drinks interval, a member of the audience asks: But what are you grieving? And I mumble some bullshit about watching a parent waste away to alcohol. Years before this reading, climbing down from the edge of a carriageway overpass, I make a pact with my future. I decide that, from this moment, my life will be an exercise in vulnerability. Writing out of that working class cycle where sadness is buried within a family, within a body, within the walls of a life.

My mother sits in a restaurant with my father and two of his friends. It's maybe a month since they started seeing each other. My father is being rude to the waiter, rude to my mother, to the point where she leaves the restaurant, followed outside by Cathy. In the busy London air, they share a cigarette. Cathy, in a quiet voice, asks if he's been violent yet. Says his previous partner left because he beat her up. My mother shakes her head, touches her belly. It is January. In a month she'll quit smoking. Come summer, in a bright garden in North London, they will announce the pregnancy.

To sit opposite your mother in a room many years from violence. To tell her you believe you shouldn't have been born. To ask her, knowing what she knew, why she went through with it? To feel the walls around your bodies, history clenching its fist. To love your mother. To hate her for bringing you here.

My father cracks the curtain of his bedroom. It is 2pm. A grey Tuesday of suburban back gardens. He thinks about killing himself. He thinks about his kids at school, eating the packed lunches he made. About his partner at work in a different city. He misses her body. Wants to share a bed with her again. Since he cheated, since she searched his wallet, found the train ticket to Didcot, called him out in front of the kids, she sleeps on the floor of their youngest's bedroom. He thinks about that night. What happened after. Coming home from the pub. Breaking her nose with a swift punch. He looks down at his right hand. He gets out of bed. Downstairs he finds a jacket on the floor. Towels draped over the arm of a sofa. Two cereal bowls half-full. He tidies up. His kids will be home from school soon, hungry as they always are. He begins to make sandwiches. He slices bread, spreads margarine. He does this every day.

Six hours pass between the moment your mother sprints downstairs waving the train ticket, and the moment he breaks her nose. Some nights you lie awake, imagining these hours stretched into thousands of seconds. Stretched this far they cover everything you are learning to love. They settle on your body, burning up on the skin above your top lip. You wake to a scream. In the morning your mother wears sunglasses. You don't see her eyes for a week.

After the launch of my first book, I sit in a pub drinking with a friend. During the launch, I read some new work, an early extract of *Before Violence*. My friend and I talk about our bodies. Each of us is covered in tattoos. My friend shows me her hands, her arm. I show her my leg. I tell her how I can't stop getting tattooed. My friend says how common it is for survivors of violence to seek ownership of their bodies through tattoos. A penny drops then, through the pool of my body, and I thank her.

I am reading memoirs written by the sons of terrible fathers. These fathers are typically terrible. One memoir begins with a traffic jam, the father impatient to the point of swearing, punching the steering wheel, violence I'd witnessed in the fathers of my friends. I never finish these memoirs. I don't want to be the hero of any of this.

Beyond the horizon of the snow lake thinning into bright silence is the playscheme you worked every summer of your undergraduate degree. Beyond that the train tracks where your friend lay down. The police report said he climbed the chainlink of the playscheme. You take the baggy of pills out of your pocket. Launch it into the sky. Watch it disappear through the lake's white roof.

When the hooded boys from the other school cross the car park. When your friends, all stoners, most of them middle-class, go silent in their True Religion jeans. When your trainers touch grass and it's just you on that riverbank. When the smallest one, a boy called Kane, swings a kick that you check with one of your own. When you resist the urge to piss yourself, to jump backwards into rushing water. When you think of your dad gripping you hard by the collar: Don't be ashamed to be scared. The most terrified dog is always the most dangerous.

In the dream your sister is climbing up a mountain. She's middle-aged, decades older than you know her to be. The higher she climbs, the older she gets. There's a distinct lack of weather in this dream. The wild grasses are still. A bird flaps its wings and she hears every feather rake the air. Soon she will be an old woman. In the distance is Ireland. Family she'll never meet.

Throughout my relationships are my parents' relationship strewn on the shore. I walk the beach, aged 29, watching the pattern unfold again and again. Here is a seagull pecking a shell. Here is driftwood smooth as bone. It's not that I believe I deserve the violence. More that the violence is the home my body knows. The home my life has made for my body. I facetime my sister, who always finds these steady men. I show her the yellow bruise above my eye, the foundation I have borrowed to cover it. Could you see it coming this time? I say yes. Will you leave her? I nod, knowing I won't, not yet.

At Glastonbury Festival your partner wakes you up with a punch to the face. In the morning she says nothing as you work the ticket booth together. Every ten minutes or so, when there's a lull at the gate, she pinches you hard on the arm. It's subtle, the way she pinches, her hand slipping back up her sleeve the second after. You say nothing. That night, you call your mother. You're blackout drunk, crying under a tree at the edge of the Pyramid Stage. You apologise for never understanding the abuse, why it took her so long to leave your father. You understand now, you think. Months from this festival, in a bright London park, your partner will cry, appalled at the things she has said, the things she has done.

The green middle of your twenties when some part of your father still wanted to live. You're cycling east to a garden where your father, four weeks sober, kneels beside a drill of potatoes, bald head gleaming in the sun. He gives you a tour of the place. Says he's in the program now. Has a keyworker. Comes here twice a week. He introduces you to Sara who offers a strawberry. Next is Gareth who looks your age, patting the soil around a sunflower. Finally, your father ushers you into a greenhouse, tells you to close your eyes. Left or right hand. You choose right. A palm of chili seeds you will plant together.

When your nana dies it is sixteen years since you last spoke and you are writing poems about her. Your dad never allowed you a relationship with his mum. Once in a blue moon she'd turn up with presents, car boot sale junk, and he'd be brutal, tell her to fuck off on the doorstep. In quieter times, when things were mellow in your family, you'd ask about her, and mostly he'd tell you to mind your own business but once in a while he'd say how her weapon of choice was an iron broom handle or how she wore miniskirts when she dropped him at school and his mates thought she was his older sister. This was before he found her in the bath one Christmas Eve. Before he and his brothers were moved into care. Before every Christmas was cast in the shadow of that event. Before you sat together at the funeral. Your atheist dad reciting every prayer the priest spoke.

Imagine your father naked in his bathroom. Ceiling light blinking. Pink shower curtain long ripped clean of its rail. Crumpled like a body in the bath. Blood on the wall from his latest fall. Imagine he stands there for a second. Opens the cabinet. Holds the thin packet of diazepam pills. Imagine he pops an extra pill. Three instead of two. Imagine he does this dry. No water. Before closing the cabinet. Imagine the click of the cabinet door and the silence after. When his prescription runs out a week early, when withdrawal arrives real as the morning he swallowed the lot, who does he imagine will be there to save his life? To put him in nappies? To lift his mouth to the light and say Dad, drink this?

Your sister calls, strung out, says it's the worst she's seen him in years. She has him in nappies. Shit on the floor, shit on the wall. The toilet's blocked and the bastard council won't send a plumber because they're saying it's your dad who's blocked it, even though the flush has been broken for months. As she speaks you feel the distance between your bodies. You are hundreds of miles away on a writing retreat in The Lake District. The retreat is part of a literary prize you won for a book of poetry you wrote about your dad. All week, from this remote cottage, you write poems about him. You leave on the first of the month. The day his prescription comes through.

The story about my father who, atheist as they come, anti-Catholic as any Irish person born in the 60s, opens the screen door of his Kilburn rental, steps onto the grubby paving stones for a cigarette. The garden is narrow. Bin bags line the fence. My father kneels through the grey air, takes a long pull on his cigarette. 200 miles away, his father has just died. Cirrhosis of the liver. My father doesn't know this yet. He ashes his cigarette. It's not clear exactly when the angel lands in the garden. My father could never explain this part of the story. He'd go quiet, look down at his pint before finishing. But the way he knew the angel was real. And not some kid, some neighbour playing a trick. Was when the sun broke through the clouds, casting everything in this sideways shadow, and the angel was clean. Below the angel, pooling at her feet, was just light. And with this he knew his father was dead.

I think about assimilation. I think about middle-class spaces. We're out for lunch, some new Argentinian joint on the Cowley Road. I've already made the decision to become vegetarian, but my father calls the shots and I don't want to disappoint him so here I am tucking into everything grilled. Under low light we play along, hiding in plain sight. Until my sister drops her fork, and he screams at her, sends her to stand by the picture window at the front of the restaurant. Everyone stares. We are a spectacle again. My sister's shoulders bounce up and down as she cries quietly, her body backlit by the busy Saturday street.

I am 26 when I get my first salary job. Home for a weekend I sit in the pub with my dad and his mates, all of them aunties and uncles of my childhood. They buy me Guinness, congratulate me. My dad keeps calling me a diamond. And it's subtle, the change that happens here. The way, over the coming months, he starts calling me middle class, dropping those two words into conversation. It reminds me of the way he'd occasionally call me camp when I was a kid. When I was getting up from the sofa. Or pulling on a pair of trousers.

When you graduate from university it is the hottest day of the year and your father is high on benzos. In his suit and tie he moves as if underwater as you pull him from pillar to post across the bright courtyard. You introduce him to friends and tutors. One professor mentions the ceremony, makes light of what your father did, how he boomed your name from the back of the auditorium. Not once but twice! And louder the second time! An echo in reverse. As if you hadn't heard the first time. As if for all the world you were a child again and he was calling you in from the street.

To think about this notion of saving someone from themselves. To think about the future and all its history imbued. Every time my father got sober, it felt as if I had saved myself from him. For a few short weeks he'd drink lime soda, and in the streets of the world I had a future. Selfish, really, to want to save someone in order to save yourself.

When your mum says goodbye she removes her sunglasses and you see her eyes for the first time in three days. She promises she'll join as soon as she can. It'll be like a holiday, she says, smiling as your sister begins to cry. She makes you promise to keep each other safe. She makes you hold hands. I want you to hold hands for as long as you can. It's snowing as the train pulls away from the platform. You are to spend Christmas with your grandparents, far away from the violence. The snow falls lightly at first, then heavier and heavier.

We arrive in Glasgow late on Christmas Eve, the city almost silent, the night holding its breath. Our grandad carries us from the platform to the car, one shoulder each. The snow comes over his ankles. We hear it creak as he walks. In the morning our Oma will zip up our puffer jackets, pull down our hats. In our mittens we'll step outside. Happiness we'll almost believe we deserve.

I am back home for Christmas, drinking in a pub with school friends, people I've not seen in years. One friend offers me coke on a key. Says he's dealing now. Inherited his brother's line. Takes me outside to his blacked-out Range Rover. We sit in the car, heater blasting, windscreen going crystal clear. I joke with him: You sure this isn't a lease? And he leans across to the glove box, produces paperwork, receipts. I ask after his family. He tells me his dad died in the summer. An overdose. Alone in his flat. Got to the point my friend was waiting for him to die. I say how sorry I am. How I'm waiting for my dad to go too. And he's laughing, in his puffer jacket, tears in his eyes when he turns to me: Remember that Christmas I stayed round yours? When my dad broke my nose? Kicked me out? And your parents let me stay over? Christmas fucking day. I thought about that this morning. When I was washing my boy's hair. When I was drying his body.

Childhood remembered by a body as a trip to the beach. And instead of sand, sky, sea etc., what's actually remembered, what this body is able to pull to the surface of itself, is the journey to the beach. The taxi outside with the meter running. The body panicking inside a jacket, unable to do the zip up. There is a kind of love here, too, in the small morning of this remembered body. Inside the family that never stops going to the beach. No matter how heavy the rain. No matter who chooses or chooses not to delete themselves.

There's a scene in the film *Aftersun* where the daughter Sophie loses her snorkelling mask. Or, that's how the interaction is framed. She asks her father Calum to throw the mask to her, and he does, but there's a breakdown in communication and the mask sinks before either of them realise what's happened. We see this unfold from below, from the perspective of the ocean floor. It's an honest mistake, but it's framed by her father as Sophie's fault, as her messing around. And a familiar dread ensues, mixing with the screams of kids and seagulls: one of fear and shame in a place designed for nothing but happiness.

My sister and I are sitting on a bench at the corner of a plaza in Granada. Well into our twenties, we still have no idea how to deal with happiness. Which is to say: we have no idea how to act when we're supposed to be happy. This is our second holiday together. We've overslept, bickered, walked in silence through heat to this shaded bench, the pair of us in need of a break and a cigarette. Across from us is a play park, complete with swings and slides and two siblings. Their father sits on the bench directly opposite us. He has this air of unflappability as he waits with his back to his kids, legs spread, arms wide, rucksack open by his side. We watch the kids go through their cycle of shout, fight, cry and the father go through his cycle of discipline. Each time he tells them off he does so with enough love to allow the kids the bravery to mess up again, to forget where they are. They are on holiday, after all. And they are children. Why should they be afraid?

I'm watching interviews with Charlotte Wells, the writer and director of *Aftersun*. In one interview, Wells is asked about audience interpretation of the film. Specifically, whether she feels the need to fill in the gaps for people. Wells says no, she doesn't. It's about feeling. It's about arriving at the feeling articulated at the end of the film. There are multiple paths to this feeling, multiple routes people can take. I type the word 'Aftersun' into the search function of social media. The film has recently been released in Japan, and the posters, covered in an alphabet I can't read, are nostalgic. I scroll past the posters to find pictures of Wells and her father on the very holiday the film is based on. Someone has taken stills from *Aftersun* and set them alongside these pictures. The two fathers wear identical white, button-down t-shirts. Paul Mescal, who plays Calum, is beaming a smile. His cheeks are almost as rosy as Wells' father's.

There was a body and then there was a body and then there was a body. You are standing on a platform at the end of a violent holiday. There's a sharpness to the air, like it would cut you if you breathed too hard. Your breakfast hasn't come up yet, but it wants to: a full English from the station's greasy spoon. You didn't get hit this time. Instead, you watched violence unfold from a second-storey balcony. You wheeled your suitcase around the edge of a pool. Soon, a stranger will offer a bottle of water. You're seven, maybe eight years old, throwing up baked beans on a platform.

We step out of the cinema into air thick with snow that won't settle, won't leave a trace. We haven't said a word since *Aftersun* ended. The lights came on and we blinked. The attendant arrived, asked us to leave. Outside it's my mum who speaks first: A bit close to home, right? My sister and I agree. We stand for a long time, the three of us, in front of the film's backlit poster. I start talking and then stop. Much like my childhood, I've almost forgotten what happened in *Aftersun*. The film has slipped my mind, like violence, and lives in my body now. On the poster are the pink backs of two bodies. Blue ocean stretching into blue sky beyond. My sister says the bodies look like islands. Dotted around the bodies are words like masterful, profound, unforgettable.

Autobiographical writing as vehicle for sympathy. Where the author, the protagonist, is rendered the hero of their own tragic story. I am standing in a nightclub smoking area, not quite black-out drunk, but almost there, sharing a cigarette with a stranger. We talk about family, about our parents, about anything and everything and it's scary, how quickly I begin to dissociate, peel away from my body, float up the smoking area wall, as this person, this version of me, tears up then weeps in front of the stranger. I wake the following evening in a panic. Lips licked raw. Heartbeat so loud I can taste it. Doors of muscle opening and closing. I gather the duvet around me, squeeze it between my fists, press it against my skin. I try to force what I've lost back inside. All my secrets floating around outside of my body.

Just my best friend and I lifting the metal shelving unit out the front door. It's nearly twice our height and rattling as we wobble in the Saturday morning light. Twenty quid waits for us, enough for a 3.5 of skunk, stuck to the fridge with a Bart Simpson magnet and a note in my dad's handwriting: *For Joe and Jake. Take shelves to dump.* The word dump underlined. We reach the first lake, sweating. Kids are carrying boats to the water. A swimmer's pink cap bobs up and down. At the turning for the second lake, we stop. The secret lake, as we call it, where homeless people camp, where kids don't go, where the fence posts to the train tracks are bent into a hole big enough for a body. And without a word we're jimmying the unit along the lake's ragged lip. Through brambles, past condoms and needles. Empty cans of super-strength cider, the stuff my dad will turn to a decade from this morning, from this littered bank where, for the rest of our teens, we return. Sharing spliffs. Laughing at ourselves. At the boys we were. At the shelving unit like a shipwreck barely a meter from shore. An altar for all the lies we told, would tell, to ourselves and to the people who loved us. Feathered moss in the coin-brown dark.

I think about gendered violence. I think about the sound of my sister's head bouncing off the oven door. How, buried in this sound, way down in the metal chime of it, was the sound of my father's head catching the iron broom handle his mother wielded. This being the only time my father hit his daughter. And how, during the years of violence, he kept her close, kept her body glued to his. Not love exactly, but not miles from love, how he weaponised her body.

My father follows his mother by hand into a long room divided in the middle by glass. On the other side of the glass are men dressed in blue and white stripes. My father is lifted onto his mother's lap. One by one his uncles appear. First Desmond, then Martin, and finally Gerard, his favourite uncle. They speak through a wall-mounted phone. When my father's arm gets tired his mother takes the phone and it's strange to see his favourite uncle speaking without hearing his voice, without being able to reach out and touch him. When they say goodbye, my father puts his hand on the smudged glass and Gerard does the same. No matter how big he makes his hand it never stretches beyond the meaty bit of his uncle's palm. They play this game for a while. My father spreading his hand into a tiny star. His uncle laughing, willing him on.

The first time my dad lays eyes on the sea he is holding the hand of his teenage mum. They are waiting for the ferry to the Isle of Wight and he's thirsty, standing high up at Southampton docks. He wants to drink the sea, to jump in and swallow the lot, but his mum tells him no, this water's not for drinking. For years my dad will be brought to Pankhurst Prison without ever realising where he is. Summer after summer he'll be told it's a holiday. We're going to the beach. And he'll remember the sea and the sky and his uncles somewhere out there in the middle of all that blue. It isn't until later that he puts two and two together. When eventually he asks and is told, plainly, as if he'd asked for the time or for the chance of rain, about his uncles' life sentences. About the man they killed. About the axe uncle Gerard left clean in his head.

We finish the last of the coke in two lines on the back of your phone. It's 10am. Our vantage point perfect. Traffic swimming the dual carriageway below. Treetops stretched long into the distance. The sun, beyond the power station, glistens above the city we grew up in. We fuck quickly. Keen not to miss the show. The car inching back and forth. The handbrake releasing a touch when we cum. It was your idea, this morning excursion. Our night having started like most of our nights out, drinking with people from school, the stragglers who hadn't gone to uni. And it had ended, not unpredictably, with a roll-through. A friend's attic bedroom. A skylight. Chain-smoking cigarettes on a roof. Sheer morning and leathery tongue. Except today was different. The power station was to be demolished. You unlock your phone. Any second now. Any second now, you say again, gripping my arm as I lick rizla, folding the paper closed on a chunky half-spliff. We sit in silence, passing the blem back and forth, sweat from the sex gone cold. In time, as summer ends and we gather our lives around us. Make plans to leave the country and then bail last minute. Sign up for clearing, vague ideas of northern cities. We'll agree we could feel the clap of the detonation in our front teeth. The delay of a few seconds as the towers jumped silently then melted and the dust cloud lifted through all we knew, reaching the sky, the distance made dirty and golden at once.

Somewhere the windowless room my father visited weekly the year I was born. Somewhere the man who waited for him, deep inside the industrial estate. Somewhere the bus he took, the car park he crossed, the burger van with its collection of bodies. Somewhere the job he lost, eventually, when the sick leave ran out. Somewhere his allotted hour of time, the squeak of trainers on corridor. Somewhere conversations. Somewhere doors. Somewhere rooms identical and numerous as all the grey mornings of that time. Because it was always morning. My father with a baby at home. My father sitting in the windowless room, explaining how, when he held his baby, it was as if he held himself. It was as if there were two of him, twinned in the kitchen dark: the monster his father became and the monster he himself would become.

My father described the feeling of holding my body for the first time as holding weather he never knew existed. You're holding this person, he would say, this warm-blooded thing, but it's snowing inside you. Pure blowing a gale. And the worst part is, it's been snowing forever. And it's not even your snow. It wasn't your father's, or his father's before. And you don't want to give this weather to your kid. You'd do anything not to. But you know you will. Standing dumb in the hospital. Crying under white light. You know this weather will snow inside your kid too, is already snowing, fields and fields of white, and there's not a damn thing you can do about it.

Near the end of the race you do the one thing a rower should never do: look up at the big screen where the boats are projected. It's the International Indoor Rowing Championships in Birmingham. Under 9s 500 metre final. You've trained all year for this, the club having moved a rowing machine into the bedroom you share with your sister, and by the looks of it you've come third, beating fourth place by a hair's breadth. The hall is massive and echoing. Floor-to-ceiling seating all the way round. Some 100 rowing machines in a grid in the middle. You're breathing hard, tasting blood and metal. You chance a look up at the stands, spot your dad. He's punching the air, holding a video camera, his Chicago Bulls cap slightly askew. You can tell by the way he's moving that he's drunk. Not hammered but drunk. His free arm hangs around one of your coaches and he's screaming at you, trying to tell you something.

To sit with your dad at the Wetherspoons near the bus station is to look around for other kids and see no one. It's near close and all the punters look glum. You imagine catching eyes with the boy who placed first in your race, sitting with his dad, sipping a J2O through a straw. Your dad arrives back from the bar with two fresh pints and a Coke, a pack of Bacon Fries between his teeth. You smell the sweat and the alcohol on his body. Life has been going this way of late, happening to you. Over the hum of the pub floor your dad tells you how proud he is, how proud his dad would be. He's slurring his words, reaching over to squeeze your shoulder. He's telling you to trust him, asking over and over whether he's ever let you down. Joe, tell me, have I ever let you down?

At the end of the novel I haven't written yet, the protagonist's dad dies alone in his council flat, the neighbours complaining about a smell through the wall. In another version, the protagonist works overtime, night shifts at the Royal Mail warehouse, until he saves enough money to check his dad into rehab. A thing I never managed to do.

100 miles from shore my father cinches the drill string, watches as water fills the moon pool. Some nights on the rig, when the air is still and the sky sufficiently cloud-covered, standing on the topside feels like being buried alive. Not that he has ever been buried alive. But the darkness, the heaviness of the silence, is the closest thing he can imagine. 20 days on, 10 days off, posted in a small town on the northeast tip of Scotland. Back on shore there's a bar, a hotel, a strip club lit pink behind the gas station, oil tankers rolling in. Out here isn't much of a future yet, beyond the thin frame of his body, all 16 years of its history. He pulls an orange from his rucksack. The brightness of its skin makes him squint.

What if violence was only ever a means of controlling who hurt you? Sure, there will be weather. Brief snow misting the brief river. Think of that boy in your body. Dragging a chair across the bathroom floor of a Saturday morning. Lifting the razor down from a high cabinet.

It is true there was a time I believed my father would kill my mother. It is true I took a cricket bat to their bedroom one morning before school. What does any of this matter anymore? My mother grows plums against the back wall of her garden. She sits out there with the plums, smoking cigarettes long into the evening.

LATE FROM THE WATER

there was the fact of your dying

and your dying itself

all winter when your dying was young

i rowed the lake for fear of forgetting

the shape of your laugh reflected in ripples

the sky pitching a tightrope between clouds

your voice in my head in the corner of a pub

saying something only your voice would say

the feeling that the sky was here for me

that it wanted me inside it had been waiting

all my life above the horizon full of pylons

and blue whales at breaktime the sky held open

a hole in the fence smiled with a lip ring as my

rucksack snagged on barbed wire and the sky un-

hooked my body gentle as a parent the rucksack

hanging in the hole like a door

like the body of a child who didn't think to bring

the sky to school i smashed into my bully in the corridor

while eating a Ginsters he lifted me by my rucksack

cartoon style because no one was dead

in the future nothing sheer beyond his

pasta breath his voice which was the sky's voice

describing the brightest scene i ever saw

men in scuba gear in the lake diving for your body

as stated previously the cigarette we passed

back and forth was the sound of time ending

because no one had died yet the sky massive and

useless in its zip fleece pre-empting no disaster

of course i will describe the lake of course

it would be late afternoon on the final weekend

of August we split the festival into sections

we agreed the water was a roof the sky walked across

how shallow the water how shallow indeed

our rucksacks forever too big for our bodies

my 28th birthday outside the Southbank

you were wheeling my bike ended up on the floor

perhaps it was the sky who landed when you fell

and the bottle of gin smashed in your rucksack

i said you were in year 7 on account

of your massive rucksack and your small body

the gap of time between

your leaving the rave and your being found

it was a Thursday late in the century the sky carried

our friendship past the far end of the car park

to the east of England the Jurassic Coast

known for its fossils people came

for miles to hunt for the bodies

of long dead creatures buried in the cliff

i was a skinny year 7 with a pen in my mouth

watching older kids emptying out of a hole

in the top field the lunch bell like a siren

one kid threw up in a bin come to think of it

i'm sure it was the sky who threw up in a bin

barely a metre from the classroom window i day-

dreamed out of biting hard on the end of a pen

until the plastic cracked and i tasted red ink

my bully with the shaved head and cut wrists

on holiday in Tenerife the sky was building

a mood board tracing the years back to a weekend

in Norwich we drove to a shipwreck

after the bender you produced from your pouch

weed gummies in the shape of cherries

the fact of your dying not fathomable even when

we asked the sky to please stop raining

so we pulled up our hoods and made a bridge

of our bodies the sky with no dying

to speak of produced lighter baggie pipe

for the duration of a half-term afternoon

we imagined our bodies safe for decades

wrapped as they once were in the arms

of our mothers snug beneath roof tiles protected

from the greedy sky the last piece of night you saw

the sky's voice long with silence arteries wide
enough to swim through you had been missing
four days when my bully called my name
put down his can of Rubicon mango
it helped to pretend you could swim
perhaps this new silence was the distance
a body could float in so many days
or the time it takes a person to survive

my bully drinking the sky outside the science block

jam sandwich breath misting the mirror

as i washed my sticky face i imagined

the darkness inside a blue whale artery

it helped to imagine you

front crawling in the blood-river of a planet

near the beginning of our friendship

i was so proud i thought about you nonstop

the relief on Sunday at the festival

when word of a security guard seeing you

reached our circle of tents your tent

as you left it quiet as a cathedral will you forgive

me when i say i got drunk that night

ate two servings of mac and cheese

as fireworks crashed over the lake

which by then had become a sky of its own

not a lick of my bully in sight

on a drive back east Canary Wharf

like a factory in the distance you told me

how you didn't like photos as means of

recording events how you preferred a diary

how you wrote three things each day

and today you would write drove home with Joe

it was near the beginning

the sky with the night in its pouch and the lake

on its breath i was flicking through channels

every station a celebrity funeral the way

your dying went viral many miles from

your laugh or the way when you spoke

you lifted your hands skywards as if rearranging

constellations there were statements

i won't put words in your mouth

unequivocal goneness the day after your body

was found i drove to Watford to buy a kitten

we talked about children imagined ourselves

fat as husbands some future years from now

our daughters further up the beer garden

you didn't want kids or at least not

any time soon i was holding the sky's

heartbeat readying a scream

at times the kitten felt like a child i had lost

in a previous life approximate closeness

holding her body on the landing

was to hold a heartbeat quicker than my own

sometimes our heartbeats landed

on the same click and sometimes they were

just off like jazzy high hat trills little breakbeats

like a pair of axes chopping the same tree

the first time i pulled a whitey at lunchtime

two hits from a Sprite bottle thick with smoke

an older kid burning the hole for the blem

called the contraption a lung i slept

next to my vomit the sound of kids

hopping the various fences it was dark

when i woke my body

curled like a cat at the feet of the sky

beyond the small morning of this

remembered body everyone leaving but no one

really gone it would be something to know

you didn't suffer but of course we can guess

the firemen laughing as they pulled on

scuba gear i asked if they had any information

the festival director clapped his hands

said thank god your friend isn't in the lake

over and over the details of your leaving

of your asking specifically to leave

the sky at the end of a growth spurt

licking rizla closed on a chunky half spliff

double maths would follow we shared

an orange on the walk across the windy field

my bully no longer taller than the sky

your laugh no longer taller than the room

inside your tent a pair of jeans bunched

into a pillow your head would never sleep on

to know without knowing that the sound

of time yawning was the shape of your body

through crown glass dressed in the outfit

you would have worn to the reading

we would have done together on the Sunday

at the festival the day after you went missing

and from the buttocks of summer the sky

concocted a plan to rob three bottles of WKD

you would have liked this story from behind

the lip of your pint the sky dropped a bag

of coppers near the security guard i walked

calm as a punter through the automatic doors

so many questions if given the choice

would you be the sky or the boy

another time the sky came up trumps

i was dared by an older kid to rob

a pair of white Air Force Ones i swapped

my beat-up shoe for the display piece

returned to school the following morning

with one fresh white trainer proud as a milk tooth

at the end of my jeans the older kids clapped

my bully had long since stopped growing

a quarter ounce of weed in a tin of mints

we passed around the IT room until

the teacher asked for the tin the sky

looked bashful handing over my sentence

on the topic of stories i never told you

outside the headteacher's office

my head of year asked why if i had nothing

to hide was i so jumpy as she opened the tin

the dead can't speak so i guess

that's the narrative

returning from exclusion it was my job

to clean the fish tank in the headteacher's office

scrub the sides and hoover up the gunk

so the fish could see beyond their world

i watched the door for a long time

after you closed it i'm still watching

still expecting you to bowl into the Southbank

late as a king with a bottle of pinot noir

under your jacket you didn't like photos

so we never took any my bully took a swing

cut his knuckle on my braces sifting for gold

in a drawer three months after you died

i found blurry photos from your launch

silly poses because no one had died

someone said you joined the 27 club

this is the thing your death became

a cultural event far removed from your laughter

by the light of a Nokia i learned how to

backskin a spliff no extra paper no wastage

by my estimation there would be a person

who heard your laugh last the sky

that lucky bastard your laughter's keeper

to watch your death from the middle

of its happening the sky pierced my ear

with an empty red biro it was Monday

at the back of the festival waiting for news

at this point it was assumed you would

turn up in need of love the sky wanted to know

if the authorities were taking it seriously

someone said your poems happened to you

at the burial yours was the only grave

on that hill we placed white roses on your coffin

the only semblance an Arsenal scarf

other than that you were hard to find

for days the specifics of that night a moment

early on when you danced a choreographed twostep

that surprised even you it appeared to come from

somewhere long before your body

did the fish in my head teacher's office

catch wind of your dying by the time

it was November i was in goal my bully

pulled a knife on the sky in order to make

your dying feel real i visited your grave

alone i wanted that place to feel

like more than a hole in the ground

your grave by then surrounded by new graves

of course we didn't watch your dying

from the middle of its happening that was

the sky's job but it was ours to live with it

alone at your grave i thought about geese

our last conversation was about migration

of all things perhaps a person walking

near the lake mistook your splash

for geese landing i'm sorry i didn't hear

as if the dance had happened a decade ago

it was time for your dying to believe in itself

but of course it was never time i bumped into

my bully on holiday in Butlins our parents

insisted on dinner together my bully and i

in the arcade in our baked bean vests

from his pouch he produced

endless tokens he shared with me

your body constellating in various

pitches of laughter a year on

you couldn't be gone it was Saturday night

we broke into school turned all the bins

and benches upside down come Monday

perusing the playground we saw our work undone

the sky was correct to proclaim we didn't matter

maybe we dreamt the whole thing

a dream of water cool as the other side of a pillow

there are things we don't know

and things i can't write maybe the lake

was in you the whole time the sky

cycling through various hues of knowing

we thought you were off on a bender

i swallowed a sleeping pill woke up thirsty

at the top of the sky

something of the sky in the way you listened

it would be romantic to say our time

was always profound mostly it was stupidness

in pubs driving back from Norwich

the pair of us hungover and squeezed

into my ancient Astra you needed a piss

no layby in sight i pulled over flush to the carriageway

i have secrets that died with you

as if your death had begun before

that of your body the sky with no future

in its pocket strobe lighting on your face

another of our last conversations

sitting on a wall in view of the Thames

your book was finished

you wanted the cover to be

the colour of water

way back when the colour of sky
depended on the colour of the water
that lived beneath it in the context
of the festival the lake was an ocean
the sky holding a snow globe with all of our
bodies inside the first time i saw a kid
sniff glue at the back of the science block
the sound was like geese landing

over the waves came the sound of your no longer being here

which was the sound of rain stopping in reverse

like any lake there would be a first time

for everything the water accepting the future

beneath the moody sky no longer

complicit in the short blue morning

of your dying i went for a piss

no music from the direction of the lake

for the duration of a physics lesson

i scratched the word sky into a work bench

i was stopped at the school gates

by the deputy headteacher

who made me sand the sky from the wood

in the direction of the year rings

oil it blonde even then he was an old man

i wonder if he outlived you

we were kids smoking weed

between the fingers of a giant's hand buried

to the knuckles each finger we scratched

our names into was taller than our bodies

we imagined the buried giant to be miles tall

in this way your life resembled the giant's fingers

for 27 years you did your thing

the future so much further beneath our living

the sound of rain stopping in reverse

which was not the sound of rain starting

or laughter somewhere about to happen

to clarify the giant's fingers were a sculpture

kids made bonfires between the various degrees

of blame surely no body was buried in that ground

in time we would learn graves can be made

in the most innocuous of places

graves can be made for the most innocuous of people

you absolutely were not supposed to die

all along the sky was bottling your laugh

for a rainy day i searched my phone

for any semblance a few voice notes

a video in a pub the week before the festival

you asked a stranger to punch you in the stomach

i have watched this video hundreds of times

another place i searched was the silence

between weathers the sky explaining how

each second between lightning and thunder

comprised a mile it was hard to hear distance like this

silence making its way towards sound

the silence between your leaving

and your being found was actually

just silence because we never heard your laugh again

across the top field older kids bowled over

on bikes to our summer smoke circle

it would go like this always a nasty one

would ask to look at our weed

then pocketing it would say that's mine

before a nice one offered us

draw on his spliff as recompense

we accepted in hot embarrassed silence

always the sky with mumbled threats

watching older kids cycling topless away

next time would be different but it never was

no matter what your life was ended

the sky slapped the daylights out of

a younger kid it was at that time

on that blue bus stop morning of mornings

i understood we were grown now

but surely we would never be grown

so long as we died before summer ended

at the restaurant i ordered

three of your favourite stews

despite the server's scepticism

how best to explain to this person

that tonight i had three bodies to feed

mine the sky's and of course your very own

and from the buttocks of my rucksack
came the sky and every lake beneath it
a kid chewing on a biro asked the teacher
for the smallest amount of water a person could
drown in this kid with an older brother at home
legendary around school who had convinced us
it would take three teaspoons
one for the mouth and one for each nostril

yours was the talent of dying to become

both everywhere and nowhere at once

all of your body soft bopping in the middle

of the dance it was a night of a million motives

my bully dressed as an iceberg

all of his future beneath the surface

a little further along the wall

even the sky was our age once

death in the form of a flood we escaped

through a door into living for a time i woke

on my knees in the bathroom the taps running

a pillow crumpled in my hands

some nights i believed the pillow

was a person i dipped for baptism

others it was a body i lifted

late from the water

all our sorrows even when

they flowed beyond the stippled ceiling

we purported to understand even

recognise ourselves in their departure

but when a friend goes when a body

barely as old as your own fills its pockets

with stones there is only the late cab

the long swim to follow

not forever exactly but the way time ends

in water its closed surface

a constellation of blue whales sleeping

way back when our collective understanding

of sky was the very end of distance

sunrise on the fifth day the sky lifts an edge

opening like a roof to a room of water

below which the body

ACKNOWLEDGEMENTS

Thanks to the editors and staff of the following publications where some of this work, or versions of it, first appeared: *Bad Lilies*, *Basket*, *Image Journal*, *London Magazine*, *Manchester Review*, *Oxford Poetry*, *Perverse*, *POETRY*, *Poetry Ireland Review*, *Poetry Review*.

Thanks to the Society of Authors for the Hartsop retreat and the University of Manchester for the 2023 Burgess Fellowship.

Thanks to the GOAT, John McAuliffe.

Thanks to Gboyega Odubanjo and Rowland Bagnall, who made the act of writing this book less lonely.